How Can a Parent Find Peace of Mind?

DISCOVERY SERIES BIBLE STUDY
For individuals or groups

Few experiences are more wonderful and difficult than raising children. Solomon recognized both sides when he said, "A wise son makes a glad father, but a foolish son is the grief of his mother" (Proverbs 10:1). For this challenge, the Bible offers wisdom. Nowhere is there more realism than in the experiences of Abraham, Sarah, David, the father and mother of the prodigal son, and others. Nowhere is there more understanding and comfort than in the Father of heaven, who patiently loves and waits in the lives of His own growing children.

———*Mart DeHaan*
RBC Ministries

This Discovery Series Bible Study is based on
How Can a Parent Find Peace of Mind? (Q0804), one of the popular Discovery Series
booklets from RBC Ministries. Find out more about Discovery Series at
www.discoveryseries.org

DISCOVERY HOUSE

P U B L I S H E R S®

Managing Editor: Dave Branon
Study Guide questions: Sim Kay Tee, Bill Crowder
Graphic Design: Steve Gier

COVER PHOTO:
Mel Curtis / PhotoDisc

INSIDE PHOTOS:
Via Stock.Xchng: Pipp, p.6; Alex Woodhouse, p.10; Jean Scheijen (vierdrie.nl), p.13; Kuba Rola, p.20; Tim Rogers, p.21;
Evan Earwicker, p.37; Maj-Britt Hoiaas Lassen, p.44; Lies Meirlaen, p.47. *Via FreeRange Stock:* David Vidmar, p.28.
Via RGB Stock: sulaco229 (Robert), p.12; Amber S. Wallace, p.26; Karunakar Rayker, p.29; Gabriel Schouten de Jel, p.34;
Sanja Gjenero, p.46. *Via Dreamstime Stock Photos & Stock Free Images:* ©Velkol, p.18; © Mandj98, p.36.
Public domain: p.36

ISBN: 978-1-57293-774-1
Printed in the United States of America
First Printing in 2013

Table of Contents

How To Use

The Purpose

The Discovery Series Bible Study (DSBS) series provides assistance to pastors and lay leaders in guiding and teaching fellow Christians with lessons adapted from RBC Ministries Discovery Series booklets and supplemented with items taken from the pages of *Our Daily Bread*. The DSBS series uses the inductive study method to help Christians understand the Bible more clearly.

The Format

READ: Each DSBS book is divided into a series of lessons. For each lesson, you will read a few pages that will give you insight into one aspect of the overall study. Included in some studies will be FOCAL POINT and TIME OUT FOR THEOLOGY segments to help you think through the material. These can be used as discussion starters for group sessions.

RESPOND: At the end of the reading is a two-page STUDY GUIDE to help participants respond to and reflect on the subject. If you are the leader of a group study, ask each member to preview the STUDY GUIDE before the group gets together. Don't feel that you have to work your way through each question in the STUDY GUIDE; let the interest level of the participants dictate the flow of the discussion. The questions are designed for either group or individual study. Here are the parts of that guide:

MEMORY VERSE: A short Scripture passage that focuses your thinking on the biblical truth at hand and can be used for memorization. You might suggest memorization as a part of each meeting.

WARMING UP: A general interest question that can foster discussion (group) or contemplation (individual).

THINKING THROUGH: Questions that will help a group or a student interact with the reading. These questions help drive home the critical concepts of the book.

DIGGING IN: An inductive study of a related passage of Scripture, reminding the group or the student of the importance of Scripture as the final authority.

GOING FURTHER: A two-part wrap-up of the response: REFER suggests ways to compare the ideas of the lesson with teachings in other parts of the Bible. REFLECT challenges the group or the learner to apply the teaching in real life.

OUR DAILY BREAD: After each STUDY GUIDE session will be an *Our Daily Bread* article that relates to the topic. You can use this for further reflection or for an introduction to a time of prayer.

Go to the Leader's and User's Guide on page 49 for further suggestions about using this Discovery Series Bible Study.

1

Thoughts to Consider

A Wonderful But Difficult Challenge

Looking back, few grandparents will say that being a parent was easy. Many, however, will say that parenting has been and continues to be one of the most rewarding experiences of their life.

Others have said that knowing what they know now, they wouldn't have children again. Some well-known surveys have shown that parental disillusionment is fairly widespread. Newspaper columns and radio and television talk programs continue to show that there's probably more than a smile behind the following bumper stickers:

- **HAPPINESS IS SPENDING YOUR CHILDREN'S INHERITANCE BEFORE THEY DO!**

- **SUCCESS AS A PARENT IS LIVING LONG ENOUGH TO BE A PROBLEM TO YOUR CHILDREN!**

Behind the humor there is heartbreak, sleepless nights, and broken dreams. The tough part of this subject for any parent is that our children are so close to our hearts. Many of us will quickly acknowledge that nothing is as important as our children. More than a few moms and dads will say that nothing else matters if their children are not happy. Nothing else matters if a son or daughter is sick or hurt or afraid.

Much of this parental concern is healthy. It goes with the territory of loving enough to care about your children. At some point, however, the care can also become unhealthy. At some point the worry over a difficult child can become consuming—and a warning of a lost perspective.

Marks of a Lost Perspective

Although all mothers and fathers experience moments of parental frustration and anger, many have said they would be willing to do anything to assure their children's happiness. It's not uncommon for parents to wish they could give their own lives for the sake of their child. These are often well-meant expressions of love, and they go with the territory of being a mom or dad.

At some point, though, perspective can be lost. Although the concern and heartbreak is understandable, it's not healthy when a troubled parent lives with the following convictions:

- **It wasn't supposed to be this way.** All too often, parents idealize what it means to be a good mom or dad. Many of us have unrealistic expectations of the parenting process. We assume that if we are good parents we will have good children—now. Such hopes and assurances are not what wise and loving parenting is all about.

- **Nothing else is important.** It is possible to not only idealize the process of parenting but also to idolize our children. As important as our sons

> ## So much of our parental anxiety is rooted in unrealistic expectations.

and daughters are, they are not all-important. We cannot allow them to become the consuming focus of our lives. We cannot afford to let our children's immature choices come between our relationship with our spouse, or our own Father in heaven.

- **Our children's problems reflect our mistakes.** While we bequeath to birth children our own human nature, it is unwise to assume that our children's problems are always in proportion to our own mistakes.

In the Old Testament story of Job, a troubled man's three friends wrongly assumed that what had happened to Job and his children was the result of Job's own sin. His friends understood the moral principle that "what we plant, we harvest." But they were wrong in assuming that the problems that came on Job's family were in proportion to Job's sin.

> ## There is no rule that says our children's problems are in proportion to our own mistakes.

If in our concern for our children we become aware of our own wrongs, we can do nothing better than to admit our failures and commit to change. But it would be a mistake to think that when we change our ways our children will change as well.

- **All hope is lost.** The experience of Job helps us in another way. In time, he learned that his moments of darkness and despair did not write the last chapter of his life. In time, the God who had been so silent—for His own reasons—did speak. And He spoke with great conviction.

Many parents have discovered that the difficult times are not forever. In time, they have learned the value of waiting on God while relying on His strength to love and to care with wisdom.

 Does the Bible Promise Good Results to Parents?

One of the most quoted parenting principles of the Bible is found in Proverbs 22:6. There Solomon, the wise king of Israel, said, "Train up a child in the way he should go, and when he is old he will not depart from it." In the Hebrew language this literally says that if you train up (initiate, imbue, consecrate, or dedicate) a child in his own way (with regard for his own temperament and individual needs at each stage of growth and development), when he is old (from a word that meant "bearded" or "mature") he will not depart from it.

Some take this as a promise. Others believe it is a general rule of wisdom that expresses the amount of influence a parent has on an impressionable child. There is some truth in each view. At the very least, this proverb reflects that if you give a child a good beginning by training him in a manner appropriate to his own distinct needs, then the positive influence of this early training will remain with him for the rest of his life. He will never be able to get away from what the parent has impressed on him. That doesn't mean the adult child will always comply with his parents' influence, but he will carry the memory of their training with him until the day he dies.

Overall, the Bible shows that a mature approach to parenting will follow the example of our heavenly Father. He loved as no other parent has ever loved, while also giving His children enough room to make their own choices and mistakes.

Thoughts To Consider

STUDY GUIDE
read pages 6–9

MEMORY VERSE
Proverbs 22:6—

"Train up a child in the way he should go, and when he is old he will not depart from it."

To understand some of the basic issues related to biblical parenting.

Warming Up

What are your greatest fears about parenting? Your greatest frustrations? How are your fears and frustrations perceived by your children?

Thinking Through

1. Consider the quote on page 8, "So much of our parental anxiety is rooted in unrealistic expectations." What are some expectations you have as a parent? Would you consider them unrealistic? Why? Why should such expectations cause anxiety?

2. On page 7, we are reminded that parenting sometimes involves "heartbreak, sleepless nights, and broken dreams." Why do you think these kinds of experiences are part of parenting?

3. On page 8, we're told that "it is unwise to assume that our children's problems are always in proportion to our own mistakes." Give an example of a situation in which a parent is to blame. How does a child's freedom to choose fit into the picture?

Going Further

Refer

Look up the following verses and determine what they say about the responsibilities of parenting: Deuteronomy 6:7; Isaiah 38:19; 2 Corinthians 12:14; Ephesians 6:4; 1 Timothy 3:4,12; Titus 2:4.

1. Using the suggested definitions found on page 9, what are the spiritual and moral implications of the command to "train up a child"?

⁶ Train up a child in the way he should go, and when he is old he will not depart from it."

²¹ Fathers, do not provoke your children, lest they become discouraged.

2. Compare the positive challenge of parental training in Proverbs 22:6 with the negative warning against parental provocation in Colossians 3:21. How can these verses work together in the parenting process?

3. Several different views on the meaning of Proverbs 22:6 are presented on page 9. Taking into account the terminology of this verse and the teaching of the entire Bible on the issue of parenting, which do you feel is the most accurate view? Why?

Prayer Time ▶

Use the *Our Daily Bread* article on the next page as a guide for a devotional and meditation time relating to parenting.

Reflect

If "the way he should go" (Proverbs 22:6) means "with regard for his own temperament and individual needs" (p. 9), parents must learn to thoroughly understand their child. How do we do that? What can you do to improve being a "student" of your child?

Is your current parenting philosophy different from the one taught in Proverbs 22:6? If so, how is it different? Do you think any changes are needed in the way you parent? What changes are you willing to make?

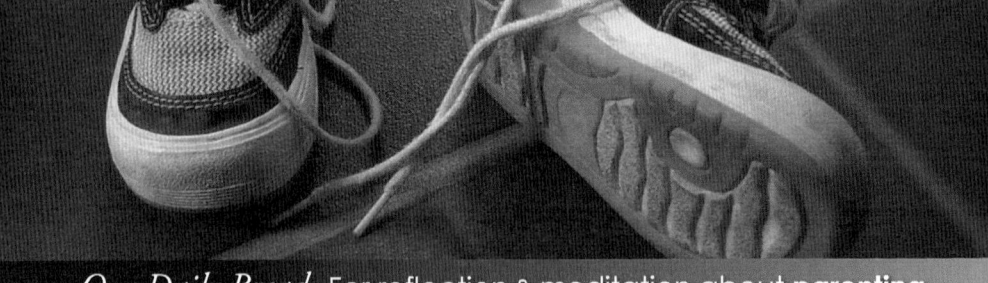

The Priority of Parenting

With parenting, there are no trial runs. We have but one chance to be good parents, and that is now. A cartoon in a magazine vividly reminded me of this. It showed a mother sprawled out in an overstuffed chair, her hair disheveled and a frazzled look on her face. Toys and crayons cluttered the floor. As her husband came in the door, he gave her a quizzical look. Exhausted, she commented, "I'll be glad when the kids are grown so I'll have time to be a good parent."

Children are young only once, and that's when they need us most! Moses told Jewish parents to seize every opportunity to convey God's laws and precepts to their youngsters—when they sat down together, when they walked together, before they went to bed, and when they got up in the morning.

If a perfect house is more important than time out for the spontaneous interruption of children, perhaps housework should be left undone. If gaining and maintaining a high standard of living leaves no time for nurturing lives, then maybe the standard is too high. Today's fast pace of life, the pressure to succeed, and the lure of materialism all conspire to sap us of the emotional energy needed to build relationships with our children.

If this is true of you, sit down with your spouse and decide today to make parenting a priority.

—*Dennis DeHaan*

PSALM 127:3—

Behold, children are a heritage from the LORD.

■ Read today's
Our Daily Bread at
www.rbc.org/odb

12

2
Guarantees, the Blame Game, and School

Accepting a Limited Guarantee

As parents who sometimes find ourselves wondering about the future, we may find ourselves wishing that God had assured us of more predictable results. It is actually more loving, however, to parent our children without such a confidence. By looking at the way our heavenly Father has loved us, we'll see that parenting is worth the effort—not because our children always make the right choices but because we've had the opportunity and privilege and peace of loving them the way our heavenly Father has loved us.

Good parenting doesn't guarantee good children. It only assures that our children will have the tremendous advantage of having had a good parent. Think about the God of the Bible. He was a perfect parent. But look at His children. Adam and Eve were raised in the best of environments. Yet they threw it all away, went the way of the snake, and gave birth to a murderer.

Then came Israel, a dearly loved nation that repeatedly and chronically became the incorrigible, rebellious child.

Then came the church, who time after time has given her Father a bad name all over the earth.

Ezekiel the prophet assumed that a good parent can have a child who turns out bad. He also reminded us that a bad parent can have a child who turns out good. He argued long and hard against a deterministic relationship between parent and child (Ezekiel 18:1–28).

By looking at the way our heavenly Father has loved us, we'll see that parenting is worth the effort.

This "tension of the exception" runs against the grain of what we often expect in parent-child relationships. When we see a child from a good family turn out bad, we are inclined to think that there must have been a dark side of parental neglect somewhere. That might be. But what about the children who come from troubled homes and turn out great? Are we as quick to think that there must have been some redeeming and determining parental virtue that we didn't see? Or are we inclined to think that the child rose above his roots and decided that he was going to be different?

It is painful enough to bear the concern that loving parents feel for the well-being of their children. It is enough to realize that we haven't given our children as much love and patience and wisdom as we wish we had. It is all the more pathetic, therefore, when we are robbed of our peace by wrong thinking.

"There is a generation that curses its father, and does not bless its mother."
—PROVERBS 30:11

It is regrettable when parents experience false guilt because they believe that if they do the right things their children will always turn out well. The truth is that if we do well, our children will be blessed with a good foundation.

Learning How to Play the Game

Tennis can be played two ways. It can be played with the kind of sportsmanship that is gracious in winning and gracious in losing. Or tennis can be played merely for the win and the money. The latter is the legacy of some of the pros we have watched in the history of tennis who have marred the dignity of the game with their center-court tantrums, profanity, officials bashing, and bitter excuses.

Parents have similar options. They can concentrate on developing their own self-control, skill, and reaction. Or they can try to divert attention from their own weaknesses by blaming others for their problems. With the latter approach, parenting crumbles into excuses like, "These kids are driving me crazy. They make me so mad. Sometimes I think I'm losing my mind. I know I shouldn't yell and scream, but I can't help it. They bring out the worst in me. Besides, I think a lot of my problem is that I came from a dysfunctional home. I can't stop yelling and hitting and arguing with those brats. I just don't have it in me."

Our first parents started the ball rolling in the blame game. Adam blamed Eve. Eve blamed the snake. The devil-snake undoubtedly blamed God. But God held Adam responsible for his choices. He made Eve accountable for what she decided to do. The snake didn't get off the hook either.

Today, we are inclined to say that our parenting problems are the result of our own parents' mistakes. There may be a lot of truth to that. But a long time ago, the Lord taught His people not to blame others for their own choices. He objected to a proverb used to diminish a sense of personal responsibility for one's own actions:

The fathers have eaten sour grapes, and the children's teeth are set on edge (Ezekiel 18:2).

Again, that's not to say that God denies the problems we inherit from our parents. The Scriptures certainly allow for the existence of learned or biologically inherited dispositions. God said:

I ... am a jealous God, visiting the iniquity of the fathers on the children to the third and fourth generations of those who hate Me (Exodus 20:5).

The Scripture also shows, however, that being under the influence of our own parents does not suspend responsibility for how we choose to respond to that influence. It is up to us to choose whether we will unconsciously follow the example of our parents, consciously aspire to it, or deliberately choose another path.

An immature adolescent son may push us to the limits. An alcoholic father or neurotic mother may hover in our memories. But none of them gives us an excuse to be adolescent, angry, argumentative, or abusive in our behavior.

 # Going Back to School

Just about the time we think we have our education behind us, along comes a strong-willed, 25-pounds-and-growing toddler who quickly pushes us to our wits' end. Suddenly we find ourselves "back in school" again. We begin to realize that parenting isn't just a matter of slowly dumping our accumulated knowledge into fresh, receptive, moldable, hungry minds. Once again we begin looking for more answers.

We develop a new perspective of "the blank slate" view of childhood. As we pick up the chalk of parental wisdom, we find that the blackboard has become greasy and unaccepting of our enthusiastic desire to write and teach something wonderful. This resistance to our teaching will last for as long as we have our children. We will find, to our disappointment, that with few exceptions they learn best when we are looking the other way.

This isn't the way we wanted it. We thought a child should be a fresh and empty document onto which we could transfer all of the knowledge we wish we had taken to heart when we were their age.

Yet learning is occurring whether we realize it or not. We are finally learning to understand our own parents. We are finding out what it's like to desperately love a little one who seems determined to mimic our faults while resisting our values, expectations, and dreams.

We are learning something about the heart of God, which overflows with love for the little ones bearing His name and likeness. We are learning something about His joy. We are learning about the pain He feels when He sees His children turn away from His loving correction (Isaiah 1:2).

We are learning a lot about ourselves. We find that these little ones are bringing out the best in us, and the worst. But even the worst isn't all bad. Our frayed nerves, anxiety, and anger can do the same thing for us as a headache or a fever. The temptation to shout and scream, or throw around our parental authority ("Because I said so, that's why!") are symptoms that must not be ignored.

These reactions tell us that we still have much to learn about what God can do in us. We need to grow in His insight, His self-control, His ability to move us with dignity through the challenges of leading a little "center of the universe" to maturity. In the knowledge that this is good for us, there is peace.

Guarantees, the Blame Game, and School

STUDY GUIDE 2
read pages 13–17

To see some of the difficulties of parenting and how to prepare for them.

MEMORY VERSE
Exodus 20:5—

"You shall not bow down to them nor serve them. For I, the LORD your God, am a jealous God, visiting the iniquity of the fathers upon the children to the third and fourth generations of those who hate Me."

Warming Up

Complete the following sentence with one of these phrases: most rewarding, most difficult, most important, least appreciated. Parenting is the _____ _____ job in the world. Which of these phrases best describes parenting to you? Why? In what ways?

Thinking Through

1. On page 14 we read about the "tension of the exception" that "runs against the grain of what we often expect in parent-child relationships." What is this tension? Why is it unexpected?

2. Page 15 tells us that "a long time ago, the Lord taught His people not to blame others for their own choices." How does the child's own responsibility balance with the responsibility of the parent to be a good example and teacher?

3. In response to Henry Ward Beecher's comment on page 17, what have you learned to appreciate about your own parents since you became a parent yourself?

Going Further

Refer

Read Ezekiel 18:1-28. What does this passage teach about individual accountability and responsibility before God? About God's mercy and forgiveness?

1. In Isaiah 1:2–3, why does the Lord refer to the people of Israel as children He "nourished and brought up"? How does this compare to the way we parent our children?

[2] Hear, O heavens, and give ear, O earth! For the LORD has spoken: "I have nourished and brought up children, and they have rebelled against Me; [3] the ox knows its owner and the donkey its master's crib; but Israel does not know, My people do not consider."

2. From the verses following Isaiah 1:2–3, how would you describe God's response to the rebellion of His children? Anger? Sadness? Disappointment? How have you responded to your children's disobedience?

3. In verse 3, the Lord said that His children had not considered (or understood) their disobedience. How can we help our children understand the need for obedience?

Prayer Time ▷

Use the *Our Daily Bread* article on the next page as a guide for a devotional and meditation time relating to parenting.

Reflect

What parenting difficulties are you struggling with right now? Do you have any parenting issues from the past that are still unresolved? Spend a few moments praying for wisdom and direction in handling these matters in a Christ-honoring way.

A Pattern for Parents

A man was having a little chat with his young son. He was trying to tell him what a Christian should be like and how he should act. When he had finished talking, his son looked at him and asked a stunning question. "Daddy," the boy wondered, "have I ever seen a Christian?" What a telling commentary on the life of that father!

How would we feel if our children were to respond to us in the same way? Psalm 78 gives us some help in making sure that doesn't happen. It sets forth a pattern for parenting—a method we can use to ensure that our children know the things of God and realize that we are people of God. According to Asaph, we can do this by "telling to the generation to come the praises of the Lord" (v. 4). When we "make them known" (v. 5) to our children, they will see by our words and our testimony that we are Christians.

Speaking of God's guidelines for living, Moses said, "You shall teach them diligently to your children, and shall talk of them when you sit in your house, when you walk by the way, when you lie down, and when you rise up" (Deuteronomy 6:7). By word and by personal example we must guide our children. In that way, we can show them and tell them what it means to be a Christian.

—*Paul Van Gorder*

Ephesians 6:4—
And you, fathers, do not provoke your children to wrath, but bring them up in the training and admonition of the Lord.

■ Read today's
Our Daily Bread at
www.rbc.org/odb

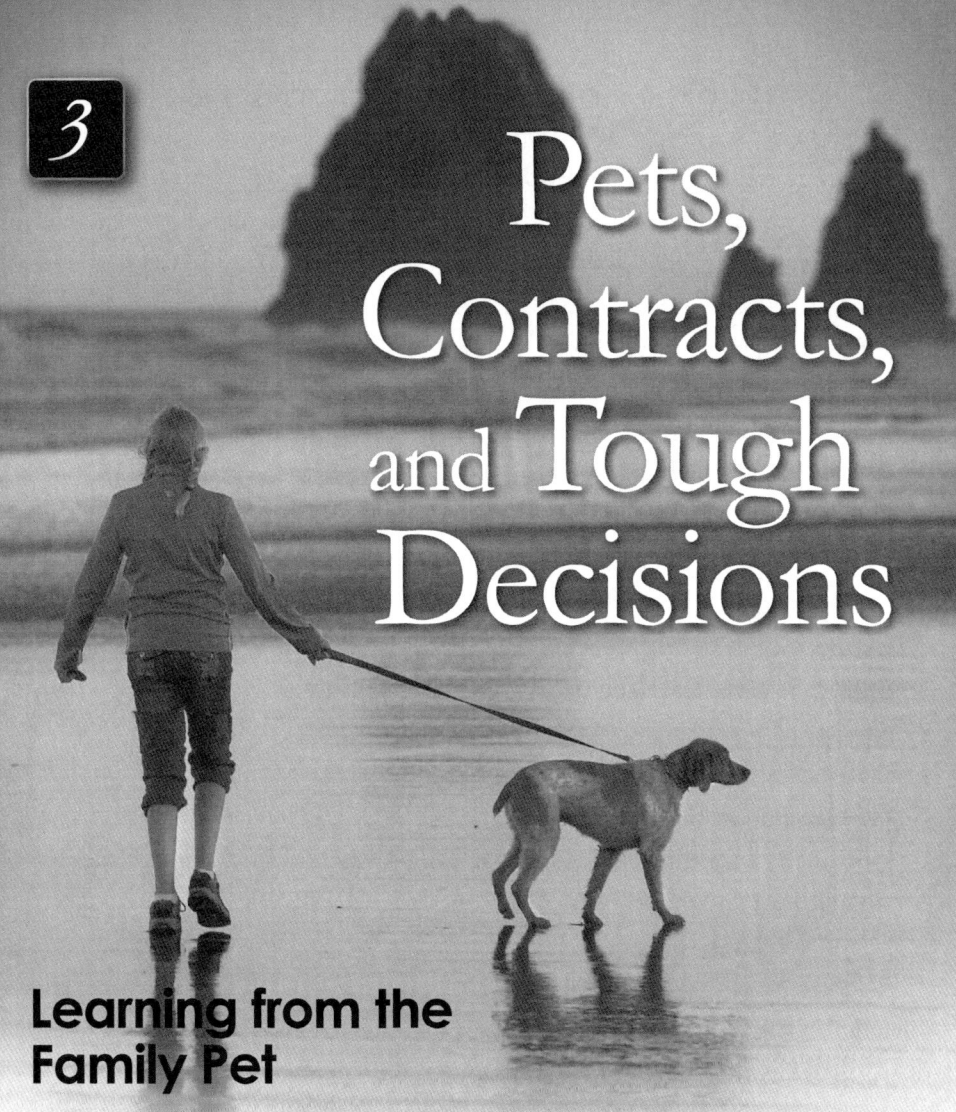

3

Pets, Contracts, and Tough Decisions

Learning from the Family Pet

Before resenting the comparison, think about it. What does it take to teach a dog to sit up and beg? How many times would you swat a dog with a rolled-up newspaper, yell, argue, or tear him down with insults? Chances are that while you might be able to keep your dog off the couch with a few swats of newsprint, the tactic would fail to get him to sit up, roll over, or bring your slippers to you. Even a dog won't learn new tricks unless you give him a treat, a hug, or warm approval.

Training a child is similar. Laying down the law, threatening with punishment, and pulling rank by saying, "Because I said so, and I'm your father. That's why!" only works for a while. After that, all the threats in the world are not apt to make your child mind. They may incite him to rebel in your face—and certainly behind your back.

Children cannot be forced to be good—not indefinitely. In time they will begin doing what they want to do whether you like it or not. The key is

There is no peace in merely laying down the law.

to help them want to do the right thing so as to adhere to God's standards and also to meet their own needs. Everyone wants to be free, to be important, to experience pleasure, and to be appreciated. Begin by helping your children to feel really cared for.

Encourage them. Spend time with them. Do what they enjoy doing. Hold them. Hug them. Do things for them that will show them that they are in your heart and that they are in your heart for their good.

Don't just give them love. Give them boundaries designed to protect their freedom. Show them what happens to people who refuse to live under the wise and loving rule of God. Find creative ways to show them that the counsel of the Word of God has been given to us to meet our deepest needs and wants.

Help them to discover the wisdom of the Proverbs, which show over and over again in many different ways that while God could just appeal to His authority, He doesn't. He gives us insight and incentive.

As a parent, you will avoid much frustration by realizing the importance of giving your children good reasons and incentives for right choices. They need to see how these reasons and incentives fit their need for pleasure, importance, freedom, and appreciation. To withhold them is to "provoke your children to wrath" (Ephesians 6:4) and to lose your own peace of mind.

 Living By a Contract

Wise parents try not to *make* their children behave. They realize that they cannot force their children to be good any more than a horse can be forced to drink water. You can lead the child to be good, but you can't make him. That's the power of the human spirit. Children who are sitting down on the outside can still be standing up on the inside.

This is not to say that you don't have to make children do things they don't want to do. There are exceptions, especially in the early years.

One of the most important lessons to be learned as a parent is mirrored in the way God deals with His children. He is a contract-making God. He tells us what will happen if we do what He tells us to do. Then He tells us, with sufficient specificity, what will happen if we refuse. He offers to help us make good choices if we ask Him for wisdom, and He readily offers to help us do anything He wants done that we cannot do on our own.

Central to the whole relationship with His children is the matter of choice. If His children go bad, it is their choice to do so. When they suffer the consequences, it is because they knowingly chose to go against His will.

The best we can do is to show our children clearly what we expect, and within what period of time. Tell them what will happen if they obey. Tell them what will happen if they don't. Then let them choose the consequences. If they

This means that we can stop yelling, nagging, and complaining.

end up being grounded, if they lose TV or computer privileges, if they are not allowed to use the car or cell phone, if they have to go to bed early, or if they are not allowed to go with the family to a ballgame—it's because of their choice, not ours.

Teaching our children to choose their own path, and then letting them experience the pleasurable or painful results of their own choices, is one of the most important things we can do—not only for them but also for our own peace of mind.

To the extent that we do this, we can stop yelling, threatening, and repeating ourselves. It means we can stop complaining and nagging to pick up the pile of clothes in their room. It means we can lower our voice and be more civilized about our expectations. It is to say, "From now on, children, you choose how it will be with you. As God fathers us, so we will parent you. We're here for you, but on these terms. It's your move."

 Bringing Our Children to Tears

We live in a day of rampant child abuse. So we have been rightly sensitized to the dangers of hitting a child in anger or using any instrument, including the hand, which might cause serious physical injury. It's just as important to realize that as a child grows up, he can be corrected by the use of previously stated consequences of his own choosing (see previous point).

That is one side of the coin. The other side is that a wise and loving parent will not be afraid to bring his child to tears when necessary. The timeless wisdom of Scripture is clear:

- *"He who spares his rod hates his son, but he who loves him disciplines him promptly" (Proverbs 13:24).*

- *"Chasten your son while there is hope, and do not set your heart on his destruction" (Proverbs 19:18).*

- *"Foolishness is bound up in the heart of a child; the rod of correction will drive it far from him" (Proverbs 22:15).*

- *"The rod and rebuke give wisdom, but a child left to himself brings shame to his mother" (Proverbs 29:15).*

- *"Correct your son, and he will give you rest; yes, he will give delight to your soul" (Proverbs 29:17).*

- *"Now no chastening seems to be joyful for the present, but painful; nevertheless, afterward it yields the peaceable fruit of righteousness to those who have been trained by it" (Hebrews 12:11).*

These can be hard words for a mom or dad to hear. In the short run, it is much easier to indulge our children than to put up with the fury of tears and complaints. In the short run, it is painful. But in the long run, lovingly appropriate and timely correction is necessary both for our child's well-being and for our own peace of mind. Often, our children are much like the servant described in the book of Proverbs:

A servant will not be corrected by mere words; for though he understands, he will not respond (29:19).

Let's pray that when we bring our children to tears it will be because of our love rather than our anger. There is no peace of mind promised to parents who bring a child to tears out of their own selfishness.

This means that parents should not give their children reason to say, "You are not being fair with me. You aren't listening to me. You are demanding more than I can give. You are never satisfied. You overreact to what I have

"Fathers, do not provoke your children to wrath." —EPHESIANS 6:4

done wrong. You refuse to admit when you are wrong. I can't reason with you. You keep changing your mind. You just use your authority as a parent. You are mean and unpredictable. I never know when you are going to blow up in anger. I'm afraid of you. You are supposed to protect me, but I need protection from you. I hate you for making me cry."

Pets, Contracts, and Tough Decisions

3

STUDY GUIDE
read pages 21–25

To see some of the tasks of parenting and how to engage them.

MEMORY VERSE

Ephesians 6:4—
"And you, fathers, do not provoke your children to wrath, but bring them up in the training and admonition of the Lord."

Warming Up

Every job has a job description. What would you include in a job description for parenting? What responsibilities are specific to either a mother or a father?

Thinking Through

1. "Don't just give them love. Give them boundaries designed to protect their freedom" (p. 22). This challenge reminds us of the balance involved in parenting. What happens when that balance is lost and a child has too much freedom—or none at all?

2. Pages 22–23 remind us of the direct connection between a child's choices and the consequences of those choices. Why are consequences so important, and what's the danger of parents protecting their children from the consequences of their choices?

3. It is valuable to be reminded that "in the long run, lovingly appropriate and timely correction is necessary both for our child's well-being and for our own peace of mind" (pp. 24–25). Why is discipline so hard for parents to practice consistently? What emotions can get in the way of appropriate discipline?

Going Further

Refer

Carefully consider the verses listed on pages 24–25. In what ways have these principles been rejected by modern culture? In what ways can they be abused by unwise or unloving parents?

1. The implication of verse 9 is that discipline done properly produces respect, not hatred or resentment, in the heart of the child. Why is loving discipline a hallmark of true parenting, even parenting as modeled by God himself?

2. When God disciplines His children, it is "for our profit" and intended to produce holiness in us (v. 10). As parents, what is the goal of your discipline? What qualities do you want to see produced in your children as a result of your loving discipline?

3. According to verse 11, discipline itself is painful. What are the results of such a painful process, and are those results worth the suffering? Why or why not?

9 Furthermore, we have had human fathers who corrected us, and we paid them respect. Shall we not much more readily be in subjection to the Father of spirits and live? 10 For they indeed for a few days chastened us as seemed best to them, but He for our profit, that we may be partakers of His holiness. 11 Now no chastening seems to be joyful for the present, but painful; nevertheless, afterward it yields the peaceable fruit of righteousness to those who have been trained by it.

Prayer Time ⟫

Use the *Our Daily Bread* article on the next page as a guide for a devotional and meditation time relating to parenting.

Reflect

Have you ever seen someone (or found yourself) disciplining a child out of anger instead of love? How did that look and feel to you? To the child? What are some practical steps you can take to protect yourself from dealing with your child in inappropriate anger?

A Child's World

A popular pizza restaurant that caters to children advertises itself as "a place where a kid can be a kid." Actually, a child should be able to be a child anywhere.

But creating a child's world goes beyond letting a kid be a kid. Parents must understand their responsibilities in guiding that child. And for that we need to look at what the Bible says about parenting:

- Parents must teach God's truth (Deuteronomy 4:9; 32:46).
- Parents must lovingly discipline children because they are immature and need guidance (Proverbs 22:15; 29:15).
- Parents should not exasperate their children (Ephesians 6:4).
- Parents' wise decisions bring blessing to their children (Deuteronomy 30:19–20).
- Parents who are godly teach their children to obey (Ephesians 6:1; 1 Timothy 3:4).
- Parents who faithfully train their children can be confident that their efforts are not in vain (Proverbs 22:6).

Above all, to create a child's world, your home needs to be a place where you serve one another through God's love (Galatians 5:13). And it doesn't hurt to have some pizza now and then too!

—*Dave Branon*

DEUTERONOMY 32:46—

Set your hearts on all the words which I testify among you today, which you shall command your children to be careful to observe—all the words of this law.

▇ Read today's *Our Daily Bread* at **www.rbc.org/odb**

Farming, Priesthood, and Fruit Growing

Working Like a Farmer

Parenting is more like farming than cooking. Good meals can be prepared in a couple of hours. And by following a recipe, you can be fairly certain of the outcome. But formulas don't work very well with children.

To get a model for child-rearing, you need to track the bread and beef all the way back to the farm where they came from. Now you're close to parenting. Parenting is far more "barnyard and back 40" than sugar and spice. Parenting is plowing and digging and raking and planting. It's weeding and cultivating and irrigating, and then waiting on the heavens until harvest time.

Depending on the year, you might have a bumper crop. Other harvests could be wiped out by bugs or disease or too much rain or not enough rain or too much heat or too much cold.

That's not to say that farming is just a game of chance. Farming can be very scientific. Put a loafer or a playboy on the farm and you're almost sure of being hungry in the fall. A good farmer is a hard worker who knows what to do with the specific crops or animals he's raising. He doesn't raise chickens like turkeys, nor corn like alfalfa. Above all, you don't see him trying quick-recipe formulas with a "sure thing, can't miss" attitude. A good farmer is a humble man. He knows his cash crop, but he doesn't presume upon the outcome. All he knows is what his responsibility is at each step of the way. If he gets a bumper crop, it's because he did the right things that were under his control, and also because the things that weren't under his control fell in line.

The apostle Paul alluded to this farming method in his first New Testament letter to the Corinthians:

> *Who then is Paul, and who is Apollos, but ministers through whom you believed, as the Lord gave to each one? I planted, Apollos watered, but God gave the increase. . . . Now he who plants and he who waters are one, and each one will receive his own reward according to his own labor. . . . And we labor, working with our own hands. . . . as my beloved children I warn you. For though you might have ten thousand instructors in Christ, yet you do not have many fathers; for in Christ Jesus I have begotten you through the gospel. Therefore I urge you, imitate me (3:5–6, 8; 4:12, 14–16).*

Paul was thinking of spiritual parenting, which is different from raising your own children. But there are strong parallels. In both cases you must do the right thing, work hard, wait on God for the harvest, and realize that you will be rewarded—not for results but for the loving nurturing you have given.

Peace of mind is found not in trying to force quick growth but in realizing that parenting is a long process of providing what our little ones need, while waiting on them and God for the results. There is no peace or productivity in trying to speed up the harvest.

Accepting the Role of a Priest

The Old Testament priest Eli raised a child who was not his own (1 Samuel 1:24–2:21). For several years, Eli acted as a parent to a young boy named Samuel. But Samuel was only a trust placed in Eli's care. In a sense, we have a similar relationship to our children. They are like everything else we have in our possession: In reality, they are not our own. Our children have been placed in our care temporarily by the Lord to be raised for Him.

In some ways, the thought that our children are not our own isn't very comforting. We know what it feels like to be concerned about returning a borrowed car or lawnmower that is worse for the wear. On the other hand, realizing

Parents can have peace of mind when they have prayed for the children God has placed in their care.

that our children are the Lord's is a very liberating thought. It means that the child's rightful owner will make sure I have all the resources I need to care for the child in God's behalf.

Parents are also like Eli in that they are like priests. In Hebrews 5:1–4 we are shown that a priest intercedes in behalf of his people, and that he does so in the awareness of his own weakness. Because he knows his own problems, he can be sympathetic and compassionate in dealing with those who come to him for help. The author of Hebrews wrote this about the high priest:

> *He can have compassion on those who are ignorant and going astray, since he himself is also subject to weakness. Because of this he is required as for the people, so also for himself, to offer sacrifices for sins (Hebrews 5:2–3).*

Since this was spoken about priests who served prior to the coming of Christ, our great High Priest, some might think it outdated. Yet, the same author also said of Christ:

We do not have a High Priest who cannot sympathize with our weaknesses, but was in all points tempted as we are, yet without sin (Hebrews 4:15).

The New Testament now calls the children of God a kingdom of priests (1 Peter 2:5, 9).

Think of the implications for a parent. It doesn't make sense for us to expect our children to be better than we were. We might long for them to make good choices. We might pray that they will be wiser than their years. But we haven't always been wise and wonderful. We've been where our children now are. We've been just as foolish, just a shortsighted, just as naive. What we have to offer them is not a perfect example, but sympathetic, compassionate hearts that continually go out to them in love and to God their heavenly Father—and rightful owner—on their behalf.

 # Growing Like Grapes on a Vine

The secret of the fruit is in the branch and root. Good parenting is the fruit of good character that is rooted and growing in God himself. The Bible calls this character the fruit of the Spirit. That is to say that it comes from the Holy Spirit of God rather than from our own natural ability or energy. Listen to what the apostle Paul wrote, and think about how it assures good parenting:

> *But the fruit of the Spirit is love, joy, peace, longsuffering, kindness, goodness, faithfulness, gentleness, self-control. Against such there is no law. And those who are Christ's have crucified the flesh with its passions and desires. If we live in the Spirit, let us also walk in the Spirit (Galatians 5:22–25).*

The reason Paul's words are so important for parents is that they not only reflect the qualities that assure good parenting, but they also point to resources of the Spirit we don't have to find in ourselves or in our own experience. If Paul is right, then our own sense of inadequacy and our own history in dysfunctional relationships can actually be put to work for us. Those can be the needs that drive us to find in the Spirit of our heavenly Father the parenting

We can't afford to forget where good parenting comes from.

qualities that are not natural to us. Listen to what Paul wrote to Christians who had been trying to live in their own strength:

> *Are you so foolish? Having begun in the Spirit, are you now being made perfect by the flesh? Have you suffered so many things in vain—if indeed it was in vain? Therefore He who supplies the Spirit to you and works miracles among you, does He do it by the works of the law, or by the hearing of faith? (Galatians 3:3–5).*

The spiritual resources of character that Paul was talking about are not the result of trying to live by the ideals of God. They come when we believe and trust what God says He is willing and able to do in us.

We need to remind one another continually that the secret to good parenting is like fruit that is rooted in the branches and roots of the Spirit of Christ. When we are in agreement with Christ and His Word (John 15:1–14), then we will be growing in our experience of the fruit of the Spirit:

- supernatural love vs. sheer effort and fatigue
- good sense of humor (joy) vs. pessimism
- calm spirit vs. anxiety
- patient attitude vs. quick anger
- kindness vs. meanness
- good motives and intentions vs. selfishness
- promise-keeping vs. breaking your word
- gentleness vs. harshness
- self-control vs. addictive behavior

Farming, Priesthood, and Fruit Growing

STUDY GUIDE

read pages 29-33

4

To see some of the opportunities of parenting and how to embrace them.

MEMORY VERSE

Proverbs 25:11—

"A word fitly spoken is like apples of gold in settings of silver."

Warming Up

What do you think is the greatest need in Christian parenting? What is the greatest threat or danger to a Christian family today?

Thinking Through

1. On page 29, we read that "parenting is more like farming than cooking." In what ways is this true? Why do we get in trouble when we try to follow a prescribed recipe for parenting?

2. We are challenged to remember that our children "are not our own" but "have been placed in our care temporarily by the Lord to be raised for Him" (p. 31). Why would this idea be disturbing to us? Why would it be liberating?

3. Consider the following statement: "The spiritual resources of character that Paul was talking about .... come when we believe and trust what God says He is willing and able to do in us" (p. 33). How does this character manifest itself in our lives? What happens when we try to parent in our own strength?

Going Further

Refer

Look up the following verses and list the various ways Paul compares his ministry to the challenge of parenting: 2 Corinthians 12:14–15; Galatians 4:19; 1 Thessalonians 2:7, 11.

1. How does Paul's description of his labor in ministry (seen in these verses) compare to the labor of parenting?

2. What emotions were being conveyed by Paul in verses 12 and 13? How do these verses parallel the emotions that we sometimes go through as parents?

12 And we labor, working with our own hands. Being reviled, we bless; being persecuted, we endure; 13 being defamed, we entreat. We have been made as the filth of the world, the offscouring of all things until now. 14 I do not write these things to shame you, but as my beloved children I warn you. 15 For though you might have ten thousand instructors in Christ, yet you do not have many fathers; for in Christ Jesus I have begotten you through the gospel. 16 Therefore I urge you, imitate me.

3. Why did Paul remind the Corinthians that he was their spiritual father (v. 15)? How is the unique ministry of a parent different from any other positive influence a child can receive?

Prayer Time ▷

Use the *Our Daily Bread* article on the next page as a guide for a devotional and meditation time relating to parenting.

Reflect

Paul's statement in 1 Corinthians 4:16, "Imitate me," is bold and daring. In what ways would you want your child to imitate you? In what ways would you not want to be imitated?

The Dead Sea Squirrels

Our family was excited to visit the Dead Sea Scrolls exhibit that was coming to town all the way from Israel. These ancient copies of the Old Testament provide evidence that our Bible has remained accurate over the centuries. Our nephew Daniel was so elated about this outing that he told his schoolmates, "Our family is going to see 'the dead sea squirrels!' " We all laughed when we heard his misquote. His little ears had turned a word he had never heard (*scrolls*) into a word he did know (*squirrels*). And in his childlike enthusiasm, he also knew that the family was going to see something wonderful!

Daniel's excitement underscores an important spiritual aspect of parenting. Values are transmitted to our children not only by what we say but by the emotions we convey. Both content and heartfelt appreciation for God's Word can be communicated to children in a variety of ways (Deuteronomy 6:4–9), including what they overhear in our conversation with others.

Young children may not initially understand each spiritual idea we discuss, but they can catch the importance we place on it. Children pick up on spiritual values and grow in understanding as we express reverence and excitement about the Word of God.

—*Dennis Fisher*

DEUTERONOMY 6:7—

You shall teach them diligently to your children, and shall talk of them when you sit in your house, when you walk by the way, when you lie down, and when you rise up.

■ Read today's *Our Daily Bread* at **www.rbc.org/odb**

5

Involvement, Selflessness, and Ending Well

Looking for Teachable Moments

I n the Old Testament, God taught His people to build rock piles so their children would one day ask why the stones were there. When the children asked, the parents were to be ready to tell the story of how the Lord of Israel had wonderfully met their needs in that place. The secret was being ready for teachable moments.

> *When your children ask their fathers in time to come, saying, "What are these stones?" then you shall let your children know (Joshua 4:21–22).*

What was the primary method Jesus used to teach His disciples?

The parent-teachers of Israel were not to be boring. They were to do things that would encourage their children to ask, "Mom and Dad, why do we do this? Why do we always have an empty place-setting at our table?" (See also Deuteronomy 6:6–9, 20–25.).

The father who wrote the Proverbs for his son realized the power of a word spoken at just the right moment (Proverbs 15:23; 25:11). He came from a tradition that used creative ways to open the hearts of children to life-changing perspectives. The Jews used education by rockpiles, by riddles, by object lessons, by drama, by word pictures, and by seeing children, over all, as being willing and active participants in their own learning.

Such child-ready object lessons are different from the kind of family devotions that are forced, ritualistic, and academic. These seldom have the desired

Making the most of teachable moments takes time and creativity.

spiritual effect. Unless our words come at teachable moments, they are not likely to draw our children's hearts toward their God. About all forced devotions do is help the parent feel less guilty about something he feels he should do.

Planning for and taking advantage of teachable moments is far better. Tender discussions about life while enjoying an afternoon in a fishing boat, a walk along a wooded field, a drive through the countryside, a spontaneous discussion during mealtime, or a tender Bible story and prayer at bedtime are usually far better received (Deuteronomy 6:6–9) and much more effective. The challenge is that you can't teach children this way without a lot of involvement and creative time spent with them.

Now, I'm not saying that we should not have mealtime devotions with our children. If it is working well and doing what you hoped it would do, then continue. But if all you are doing is trying to force your children to learn something, chances are they may be learning to resent not only Bible reading and prayer, but also you and your Lord.

 # Dying a Thousand Deaths

The most effective parents die a thousand deaths. Sometimes it is the result of being embarrassed by the actions of their children. Sometimes it is the result of utter frustration and fatigue. Sometimes it is over the deep concern of a son or daughter's shortsighted and self-destructive choices. But often these parents voluntarily die to their own desires just because this is what it takes to bring children into the world.

No one said that bringing children to maturity would be easy. It's hard for a mother to go through the contractions of labor. It's hard for her to give years of her life to infants and toddlers who constantly demand attention. It's hard for a wife and husband to give up the freedoms they enjoyed before children. It's hard for a father to put aside his strong will and give his son the space he needs to make his own decisions. It's hard to give your children

● FOCAL POINT

"Quiet times. Noisy times. Busy times. Free times. Your family has them all. Among those moments that occupy your day, you should attempt to find 'teachable moments.' These are the important minutes and seconds when your children are most ready to learn the vital principles you intend to teach them. Prepare yourself now by keeping in mind the concepts you want your children to learn. Then look for teachable moments."

—Dave Branon

more and more freedom with less and less control so that they can begin to feel the responsibilities of maturity. It's hard not to jump in and rescue them when they get themselves in trouble. It's hard to remain firm in providing reasonable boundaries and controls so they are not left entirely on their own. It would be easier sometimes to give in and get them off your back. It's hard

> ## "Unless a grain of wheat falls into the ground and dies, it remains alone; but if it dies, it produces much grain." —JOHN 12:24

to continually help them to see that the real issue is not what you want them to do but what they are going to choose and with what consequences. It's hard not to jump in and take control. It's hard to be patient enough to give them as much time as they need to grow up. It's like dying to let them go out into the cold, cruel world.

It's hard to pray for them daily. It's harder to pray in a way that reflects our surrender to God. It's hard to say to the Lord, "Do whatever it takes to bring my children to You and to maturity of faith and love, do whatever it takes."

Ironically, we are inclined to think that taking an easier path will result in less pain and more joy. Good parenting, however, is the result of Christlike character. And unless we follow Christ's lead and that of the apostle Paul (2 Corinthians 4:1–12), we will never see the difference Christ's Spirit can make in us. Only when we die to ourselves do our children get the benefit of Christ parenting through us.

> ## "Now My soul is troubled, and what shall I say? 'Father, save Me from this hour'? But for this purpose I came to this hour."
> —JESUS IN JOHN 12:27

Preparing for an Empty Nest

Empty-nest syndrome has established itself as a real dimension of mid-life crisis. Life after children is now recognized as another threat to marriages that have survived earlier tests. Parents who have lived all their lives for their children suddenly find themselves rattling around in an empty house. They become restless, unsatisfied, and irritable. Anxiety, anger, and depression can come in slowly like a fog.

If empty-nest syndrome marks yet another test for parents and their marriage, it should also be seen as the mark of success and hope for the child.

Children are not born to be children. The highest good is not to be protected and directed by hovering, smothering parents. From the day a baby is born, his parents should understand that their mission is to prepare this child to fly.

Maturity is better than immaturity, independence is better than dependence, and the day of departure is better than the day of arrival.

> "The most important thing that parents can teach their children is how to get along without them." —FRANK A. CLARK

If after working through the normal pains of departure, parents are still apt to be overinvolved, overprotective, and meddlesome in their adult children's lives, then there is a need for some housecleaning. It might be time to acknowledge and discard a pattern of selfish control and smothering. It might be time to accept the fact that we have been overinvolved, not for the child's good but to indulge our own selfish needs. It is difficult to let our children go, especially if we have become dependent on them. Dependence signals the child in us, and it is a warning that we are not finding our satisfaction and peace in God himself.

It is interesting to note the way God parents His children. In both Old

> ## "There are only two lasting bequests we can hope to give our children. One of these is roots; the other, wings." —HODDING CARTER

and New Testament times, the heavenly Father temporarily nurtured His children with a heavy provision of miraculous signs and wonders to assure them of His presence. In time, He withdrew the obvious presence of the miraculous and forced His children to sink or swim in the disciplines of faith.

God has made man and woman to leave their parents and cleave to a new mate of their own. It is in this new sphere of independent living that a person is the freest to learn to love God, parents, mate, children, and friends. It is here that we can find the peace of mind God provides.

Being Late Rather Than Never

Saying I'm sorry is better late than never saying it at all. Saying I love you is better said on a deathbed than to die without ever having said it. Finding ways to encourage your children late in life is better than letting them come to their own end wondering, "Did Mom or Dad ever really care about me?" One of the most amazing experiences is to see the good that a few words of encouragement can do even at the end of that parent's life.

There is no way of changing the wrongs of a lifetime. The human consequences of selfish, alcoholic, adulterous, abusive, workaholic parenting cannot be wiped away like unwanted chalk on a blackboard. But you can know the joys of the Teacher who taught His followers to live one day at a time, confess their wrongs, make restitution where possible, and thereby know God's peace.

But what if the child dies before the parent has a chance to show that care? You can still dignify and honor the life and memory of that child. You can put your mistakes to work for someone else who could benefit by being cared for by you.

The apostle Paul illustrated the possibility of putting our mistakes to work for others. He became like a father to many after having made many violent mistakes. In his early years, he was an angry and abusive man (Acts 8:1–3). His actions left memories that weighed heavily on him (1 Timothy 1:15). Yet he didn't give up. He went on to become one of the most important parent figures of all time. Driven by the mistakes of his past, and by the forgiving love of God, he went on to be like a father to those who soaked up his love, his wisdom, his example, and his prayers.

To finally have the blessing of a parent can be like a soothing drink of water so satisfying that you can remember that drink every day for the rest of your life.

After finding out how much God loved him, after a change of heart, and after experiencing the redeeming strength of Christ, Paul became known for his example, his advice, his correction, and his warm, affirming words of encouragement. He learned to provide the gentleness of a mother and the strong comfort and challenge of a father (1 Thessalonians 2:7–12). His "adopted" children would certainly say, "Better late than never."

Involvement, Selfishness, and Ending Well

STUDY GUIDE
read pages 37–43

MEMORY VERSE

1 Thessalonians 2:12—

"Walk worthy of God who calls you into His own kingdom and glory."

To see some of the frustrations of parenting and to examine biblical responses to those frustrations.

Warming Up

As a parent, how would you define a teachable moment with your child? Identify some everyday events that you could use as teachable moments, and share how you used one such event to teach your child about life or about God.

Thinking Through

1. Do you agree with the writer's view that family devotions can be "forced, ritualistic, and academic" (p. 38)? What has been your own experience? What are the values and the dangers of family devotions?

2. On pages 39-40 we are reminded that sometimes it's hard to pray for our children—particularly when we're asking God to do whatever it takes to bring our children closer to Him. Why is this so hard?

3. Why must "effective parents die a thousand deaths"? (pp. 38–40). How has this been true in your own parenting experience?

Going Further

Refer

The final section deals with the painful issue of reconciliation (pp. 42–43). What example of personal reconciliation in Paul's life is found in the following verses: Acts 15:36-40; Colossians 4:10–11; 2 Timothy 4:11?

What effects did reconciliation have on both parties?

1. In verse 7, Paul compares his ministry to the care of a nursing mother for her child. In the following verses (vv. 8–12), what descriptions of his ministry sound like the loving care of a mother?

2. What key words in verses 7–8 indicate Paul's relationship with the Thessalonian believers? What caring actions resulted from his strong feelings for them (vv. 8–10)? How does Paul's example apply to our own parenting?

3. Paul did three things for the Thessalonian believers "as a father does [for] his own children" (v. 11). What were they, and why is each significant?

7 But we were gentle among you, just as a nursing mother cherishes her own children. 8 So, affectionately longing for you, we were well pleased to impart to you not only the gospel of God, but also our own lives, because you had become dear to us. 9 For you remember, brethren, our labor and toil; for laboring night and day, that we might not be a burden to any of you, we preached to you the gospel of God. 10 You are witnesses, and God also, how devoutly and justly and blamelessly we behaved ourselves among you who believe; 11 as you know how we exhorted, and comforted, and charged every one of you, as a father does his own children, 12 that you would walk worthy of God who calls you into His own kingdom and glory.

Prayer Time

Use the *Our Daily Bread* article on the next page as a guide for a devotional and meditation time relating to parenting.

Reflect

As you think over this entire study of parenting, what principles are you currently practicing? What principles do you need to become more consistent in? Conclude this study by committing your children to the Lord and asking Him for His wisdom and strength.

Loving Grown-up Kids

Comedian Henny Youngman used to say, "I've got two wonderful children—and two out of five isn't bad."

When children reach adulthood, most parents have an opinion about how their offspring have "turned out." Some are proud of everything their kids have done, while other parents express misgivings or disappointment about the choices their children have made. How can we continue a positive parenting role after the birds have left our nest?

In 1 Corinthians 13, often called "the love chapter" of the Bible, Paul writes that the greatest gifts of speaking, understanding, and sacrificial service are worthless without love (vv. 1–3). Love itself is the foundation of winsome behavior, and its influence never ends. "Love suffers long and is kind; love does not envy; love does not parade itself, is not puffed up; does not behave rudely, does not seek its own, is not provoked, thinks no evil; does not rejoice in iniquity, but rejoices in the truth; bears all things, believes all things, hopes all things, endures all things. Love never fails" (vv. 4–8).

When our children no longer seek our advice, they still value our love. In every stage of parenting, it's not only what we say but what we do that counts.

—*David McCasland*

1 CORINTHIANS 13:13—
And now abide faith, hope, love, these three; but the greatest of these is love.

■ Read today's
Our Daily Bread at
www.rbc.org/odb

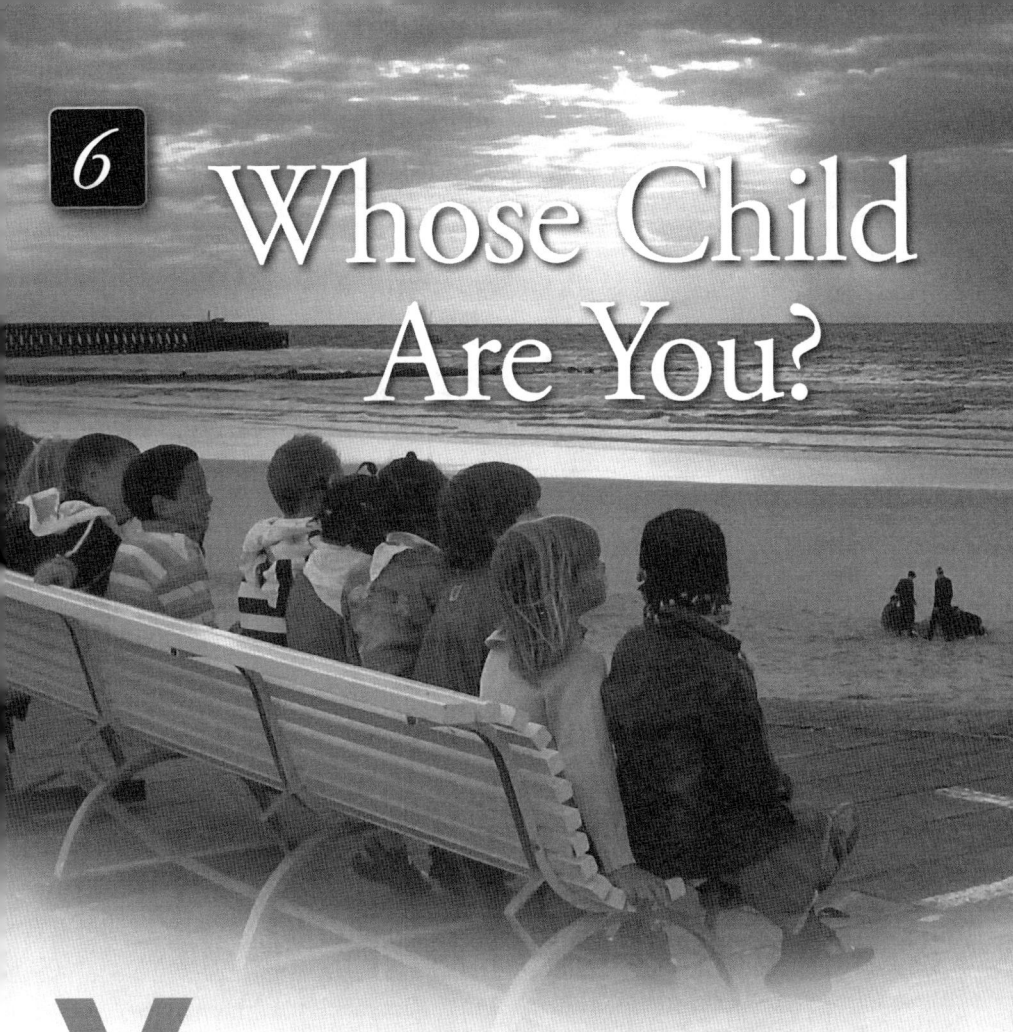

6 Whose Child Are You?

You don't have to be the adult child of a divorce, or of an alcoholic, a workaholic, or a physically, verbally, or sexually abusive mom or dad to have doubts about yourself as a parent. All of us have questions about what we are going to pass along to our children. Some of us wonder whether we are going to be able to be as good to our children as our parents were for us. The good news is that we don't have to pass along a legacy of parental inadequacy.

The God of the Bible has offered to adopt, raise, and live His life through you if you will allow Him to parent you. The God and Father of the Lord Jesus Christ has offered to adopt and name you in His eternal inheritance if you will

Not only can you be a child of God, but He can also enable you to live like one!

acknowledge your sins and trust Jesus' gift of salvation through His death and resurrection (Ephesians 1:3–12; 1 John 5:1).

In this new relationship to God, a parent can find a love, a security, and a confidence that God alone can give. It begins as we trust Christ as Savior from sin's eternal penalty. It continues as we rely on Him for wisdom and enablement.

This is the only way that "children having children" really works in our favor. When we trust God and live as His children, He will develop within us the character that is the secret of good parenting.

■ LEADER'S and USER'S GUIDE

Overview of Lessons: How Can a Parent Find Peace of Mind?

STUDY	TOPIC	BIBLE TEXT	READING	QUESTIONS
1	Thoughts to Consider	*Proverbs 22:6; Col. 3:21*	pp. 6–9	pp. 10–11
2	Guarantees, Blame, School	*Isaiah 1:2–3*	pp. 13–17	pp. 18–19
3	Pets, Contracts, Tough Decisions	*Hebrews 12:9–11*	pp. 21–25	pp. 26–27
4	Farming, Priesthood, Fruit Growing	*1 Corinthians 4:12–16*	pp. 29–33	pp. 34–35
5	Involvement, Selfishness, Ending Well	*1 Thessalonians 2:7–12*	pp. 37–43	pp. 44–45

Pulpit Sermon Series (for pastors and church leaders)

Although the Discovery Series Bible Study is primarily for personal and group study, pastors may want to use this material as the foundation for a series of messages on this important issue. The suggested topics and their corresponding texts from the Overview of Lessons above can be used as an outline for a sermon series.

DSBS User's Guide (for individuals and small groups)

Individuals—Personal Study

• Read the designated pages of the book.

• Carefully consider the study questions, and write out answers for each.

Small Groups—Bible-Study Discussion

• To maximize the value of the time spent together, each member should do the lesson work prior to the group meeting.

• Recommended discussion time: 45 minutes.

• Engage the group in a discussion of the questions—seeking full participation from each member.

Note To The Reader

The publisher invites you to share your response to the message of this book by writing Discovery House Publishers, P.O. Box 3566, Grand Rapids, MI 49501, USA. For information about other Discovery House books, music, videos, or DVDs, contact us at the same address or call 1–800–653–8333. Find us on the Internet at **http://www.dhp.org/** or send e-mail to **books@dhp.org**.